The Canadian Business

Etiquette Book Series

BOOK 1

POWER SUIT
POWER LUNCH
POWER FAILURE

LEWENA BAYER

2nd Edition. 2016

Copyright

Power Suit, Power Lunch, Power Failure

Copyright © 2016 by Lewena Bayer

Published by Propriety Publishing, 2016

www.proprietypublishing.com

PROPRIETY
Publishing

ISBN: 978-1-77334-000-5

Table of Contents

INTRODUCTION

INTRODUCTION

Some regard etiquette as an old-fashioned word. In conjures up memories of "the good old days" when everyone knew their place and acted accordingly. Somehow the perception that etiquette is only relevant for fancy situations, such as formal dinners and wedding receptions, or that it is all about arcane etiquette deals with much more than which fork to use for the salad course or where to put your napkin. In the ever-changing modern office environment, basic etiquette can teach you how to deal with almost any situation that comes your way. That's because etiquette is really about respect and leadership-taking the time to put people at ease, evaluating the needs and intentions of others and thinking before you act. In other words, good manners are critical for advancing your career in business.

The value of etiquette is far reaching: it helps build better relationships, it helps us present ourselves positively, it aids in communication and it effectuates confidence in social situations. This is particularly true in the modern office environment where gender balances have shifted, new technology has created the need for new protocol and "casual Fridays" leave us wondering how it is we're supposed to dress. Certainly, everyone can remember a time when they floundered with the guidelines for behavior in a particularly memorable business situation. Remember your first job interview? First business luncheon? Or the first time you were invited to the boss's house for drinks?

In each awkward situation uncertainty about the "rules" left us insecure and vulnerable.

This book is a clear and concise guide to basic business etiquette: how to make a good first impression, how and when to make introductions, how to deal with bosses, co-workers and employees, gender roles in business, basic tips on technology, and how to dress in any business situation. All the information in the book relates to the basic rule of etiquette, which is putting others at ease. Etiquette is simply a way to be aware of others, and to treat them as we would like to be treated. When clients or customers feel comfortable with us, they are more likely to retain our services. When a boss and co-workers find us easy to work with, he or she is more likely to overlook our shortcomings.

Finally, when a boss is able to put employees at ease, those employees are usually more motivated, more likely to remain at their jobs, and more likely to work hard for their boss and the company.

In writing this book, we the experts at CivilityExperts.com wanted to put the reader at ease. For this reason, we've included not only clear and easy-to-find information, but some fun "bad examples" too. Characters like Ivana Talkalot and Mr. Monotonous pop up on occasion to remind us that no matter how concerned with self-improvement we are, there is always someone worse off!

Finally, our goal is to bring civility back in style and make our workplaces better places to be. We at

CivilityExperts.com have been encouraged by the positive press and interest from the public in general in our business etiquette and civility workshops. We offer the In Good Company Series for business people because we firmly believe that good manners are good business.

Are you an offender?

About 96 percent of Americans have experienced incivility at work. Here's what it looks like:

– Taking credit for others' efforts
– Passing blame for your own mistakes
– Checking e-mail or texting during a meeting
– Sending bad news through e-mail so you don't have to face the recipient
– Talking down to others
– Not listening
– Spreading rumors about colleagues
– Setting others up for failure
– Not saying "please" or "thank you"
– Showing up late or leaving a meeting early with no explanation
– Belittling others' efforts
– Leaving snippy voice mail or e-mail messages
– Forwarding others' e-mail to make them look bad
– Making demeaning or derogatory remarks to someone
– Withholding information
– Failing to return phone calls or respond to e-mail
– Leaving a mess for others to clean up
– Consistently grabbing easy tasks while leaving difficult ones for others
– Shutting someone out of a network or team
– Paying little attention or showing little interest in

CHAPTER 1

FIRST IMPRESSIONS:
Will the real CEO please step forward!

The meter is running. You only have so much time to make a first impression and it goes without saying that you're after a good one. We believe you only have a short time -anywhere from 15 to 60 seconds- to make a good first impression. Therefore, time is of the essence. A polished professional is well aware of the risks he or she takes when the impact of a first impression is ignored.

How many times do you think someone has made an incorrect assessment of you based on a first impression? Even those of us who consider ourselves seasoned executives need to be aware of what kind of signals we're sending. It's pretty easy to settle into bad habits. Been losing clients lately? Wondering why your social life seems to have fallen off? Passed over twice for that promotion? Maybe you need to practice the tips and exercises in this chapter or the appendix to increase the chances of making a positive first impression. Do you know how you are presenting yourself?

Fortunately, we do have some control over first impressions. There are guidelines for behaviors, which help define your presence as polished and professional even before you have an opportunity to speak. Take the self-assessment quiz and see how much you know.

QUIZ: SELF-ASSESSMENT

1. When I am wearing a nametag it should be on my right lapel.

    True or False

2. If a man and woman meet, the man should always take the initiative and extend his hand to make an introduction.

    True or False

3. At a formal event, a man need not wear a tie.

    True or False

4. A good hand shaker maintains hand contact until an introduction is complete.

    True or False

5. When you meet someone new you should always stand and extend your hand.

    True or False

6. Gossip is a typical and harmless activity in the workplace.

    True or False

7. When introducing your boss to your spouse, you say your spouse's name first.

    True or False

8. It's easy to remember someone's name if you associate their name with an unrelated object.

    True or False

9. You have between 30 and 120 seconds to make a first impression.

    True or False

10. Even in business men should hold the door or pull out chairs for women.

    True or False

(See answers at the end of this chapter.)

A: Pleased to meet you!

Over the course of an ordinary day in the etiquette business, we meet an average of twenty new people. How many people do you meet? If you're in customer service or on the front line in your work, you may meet five times that number. If we could survey everyone you came in contact with, what do you think they would say about their first impression of you?

There are five basic and mandatory rules of etiquette for meeting someone new:

- Make eye contact

- Stand up, if you cannot stand, move your body towards them

- Smile

- Extend your hand to shake theirs

- Say hello

Making memorable first impressions is so simple. So simple, in fact, that people undervalue its importance. If you consistently do all five of the above, when you meet someone, you're at least halfway towards making a good first impression.

B: Don't roll your eyes

In most North American workplaces, an ability to make timely and direct eye contact just may be the secret to your success. When you come into a room hold your head up. Scan the room briefly to acquaint yourself with the surroundings, and then adjust your behavior accordingly. Look people right in the eye. The only exception to this rule pertains to dealings with people from specific cultures where direct eye contact is not appropriate.

It is considered very bad manners to break eye contact during a conversation, especially if it is obvious that you are not interested in the conversation and are prowling for prospects amid pretending to show interest to someone else.

If you are approached by people you are not interested in meeting, be polite, but be direct. Make eye contact, shake their hand and say hello. There is no reason you cannot politely say, "Excuse me, I hope we can speak again later," or "if you'll excuse me, there's something I have to attend to." Smile and make your exit. People recognize when they are being treated insincerely, so be sincere in greeting them but don't pretend you're interested in having a conversation and do show them the courtesy of not wasting their time either.

Throughout introductions, maintain eye contact but try not to stare. One hint is to shift your view to the person's eyebrows after a few seconds so that he or she knows that he or she has your attention but there is not an uncomfortable glaring into a person's eyeballs. We often tell young children to keep direct eye contact long enough to know a person's eye color. Whatever you do, don't let your attention or your eyes wander when engaged in an introduction.

C. Shaken not stirred!

Be safe! The handshake is the only universally accepted greeting in North America.

As you travel through different countries, acceptable greetings might change. In some places, hugs and kisses are not only suitable but also expected. In typical North American environments, business colleagues may feel quite uncomfortable when others are hugging. How often have you seen this situation or been on the outside looking in? Clients or associates wonder where to look or if any unsightly group hug will be initiated. Patting and inappropriate touching can also be misconstrued as harassment in some work situations. Better to stick with the ever safe and appropriate handshake. In

Recommended Reading: CHOOSE CIVILITY by Dr. P. Forni and SOCIAL INTELLIGENCE by Daniel Goleman

North America people will judge you based on your handshake and yes, you should always shake hands when you meet and greet as well as when you leave a situation or end an interaction.

Maybe you've had experience with some of the following handshakes:

THE DAMSEL IN DISTRESS: This is the infamous limp hand shake. Could be extended by a man or a woman. This person extends his/her fingers instead of his/her hand and seems to be expecting the kiss that will never come. Kind of makes you feel sorry for the poor little thing. No secret who's in charge here?

THE BONE CRUSHER: There's one in every crowd. The greeting turns into a competition, or the threat of never being able to use the crushed hand again. Either the bone crusher just doesn't know his/her own strength or maybe the plan is to try to intimidate you right off the start by causing bodily injury.

THE JUGGLER: This is a very annoying hand shake indeed. This person ends up extending his/her plate of chicken fingers or his/her elbow for you to shake because the other hand is holding their cell phone, or cigarettes, or knapsack and they truly don't understand the value of a handshake. By the time the handshake is finished you are probably holding the majority of this person's items, wondering where to put them.

These handshakes leave us with an unpleasant first impression, which can be avoided by following simple guidelines for a great handshake.

Guidelines for a great handshake

A great handshake tells others you are confident and at ease in your surroundings. It makes others feel welcome and comfortable in your presence. Handshakes are the most commonly accepted (and appropriate) physical contact for men and women in the North American business arena. A good Handshake consists of the following:

- Keep the fingers together with the thumb up and open

- Slide your hand into the other person's so that each person's web of skin between thumb and forefingers touches the other's

- Squeeze firmly and pump two or three times from the elbow

- Release after the shake, even if the introduction continues

- Maintain good eye contact with the other person

You should extend your hand when meeting someone for the first time, when greeting someone you haven't seen in awhile, when being introduced, when saying good-bye to someone, and whenever anyone else extends his or her hand.

Also, note that extending your arm for the purpose of shaking hands can often be just the excuse you need to interject into an ongoing conversation and introduce yourself to that "important" person you've been waiting to meet. Obviously you should not barge in and introduce yourself, but, often eye contact and an extended hand are enough to solicit a pause in a conversation. Make sure you've prepared a greeting so that you can keep someone's attention once you've captured it. This is the key to "schmoozing." Exhibiting a sense of humor and doing your research go a long way in maintaining conversation with someone new.   Usually compliments come into play and a great conversationalist understands that people love to talk about themselves so they will generally maneuver the conversation so that they quickly become the listener.

In the next chapter we'll discuss tips for remembering someone's name after you've successfully completed the handshake.

D. The art of schmoozing

Time constraints and fierce competition in the modern business world dictate that we are often called upon to make business contacts in casual, "party," or social situations. This is called "schmoozing." On the one hand, mixing business and social activities makes sense. Four or five people you need to meet are in the same room at the same time and it's a perfect opportunity to chat with them, make a first impression, and get a sense of who they are. On the other hand, the rules in these situations can be extremely complicated. How are you expected to behave in this situation and how do you make the most of it while maintaining your professional reputation?

First of all, etiquette dictates that you're far better off making a few solid and memorable contacts than you are fluttering around the room shuffling business cards like a blackjack dealer. It may seem a little contradictory, but sincerity is the key to good schmoozing. Do you homework so that you're confident, make eye contact, smile and be direct whenever possible. Call the event host/hostess to find out who will be attending the function. Map out what you hope to accomplish and prioritize those you need to meet most at the function. Keep in mind the purpose of the event, however, and be tactful. For example, everyone knows that fundraising events, while primarily about raising funds for specific cause, also serve a networking purpose.

But there is an appropriate time and place for everything. You would never approach the doctor who is presenting a keynote address on children with disabilities at a fundraising event and try to sell him a new, unrelated pharmaceutical your company is representing. However, you should certainly introduce yourself, comment on their speech, ask for their card and follow up with a sales call at a later date. Of course, if the doctor initiates a conversation about you or your company, by all means take advantage, but keep it brief and make arrangements to discuss it further at a more appropriate time and place. Good manners also dictate that you should not attend a fundraising function with the intention of schmoozing if you have not made some donation, whether time or money, to the specific cause.

Once you have scanned the room and targeted some key contacts, make your way over to them. Don't beeline and look over-eager but watch for a moment when the "targets" are alone or not seemingly engaged in deep conversation. Be polite to those you pass on the way, shake a few hands, smile and make eye contact but do not get caught up in a conversation. If you find yourself "trapped" by someone in whom you are not interested, be respectful, say something kind-"Enjoy your evening" or "do try the shrimp canapé"-to close the communication and excuse yourself.

If it appears that the person you are dying to speak with will be completely occupied for most of the evening and the host does not have an opportunity to introduce you, make your way over to the person anyway. Wait for a break in the conversation and while extending you hand say something like, "Excuse me for interrupting, Mr. Guest of Honor, my name is Miss Have to Meet You, I know you have many people to talk to tonight so I'd like to leave you with my card and ask that I may call you next week so we can talk more."

E. Non-verbal communication style: Are you the master of your own domain?

In our workplace seminars we teach our students that fifty percent of all communication is nonverbal and of the fifty percent which is verbal, more than half is quickly forgotten or misunderstood. This indicates that if your body language does not echo what's coming out of your mouth, whoever is listening is probably not getting the message you are trying to communicate. One important aspect of nonverbal communication is posture and body language. Are you in control of all your actions? If you are truly the master of your domain, you are aware of all the signals you send at any given time. There is tremendous power in understanding this. Not only can you better control the messages you send, but also you can properly read signals sent by others. Here are some people you may recognize from previous first impressions.

MISS DEMEANOR: This woman has A-T-T-I-T-U-D-E written all over her. From the stern expression on her face to her serious gestures and stiff posture, it's obvious to all she would rather be somewhere else. Don't even approach her unless you brought a sweater because she'll be venting and it will be chilly

SPARKY: This guy can hardly contain himself. Just like an excitable pooch, he's straining to break free. Either one knee shakes or one hand clicks the pen incessantly. He runs his hand through his hair constantly and the rapid "yeah, yeah, yeah" starts to sound like panting. His eyes are darting all over the room and if he's not set loose soon you might see something running down his pant leg.

MR. CASUAL: Wow! What confidence. Not a care in the world. This character acts like he's got it all in the palm of his hand. You can tell he contemplated leaving the suit jacket in the car. He's already helped himself to a handful of mints, he slouches comfortably in the boss's chair, and he loosens his tie and maybe one too many shirt buttons. He's not at all shy about scratching if he has to and if the meeting/ reception/interview go into overtime, he just might take off his shoes. Yikes!

BETTY BOOPSTER: Ooooooooo, I'm so excited to see you because I'm so gorgeous I can't stand myself...this courtesy-free cupcake flutters around the room brushing up against everyone she meets. You'll have to help her with her chair because one hand's busy twirling her hair while the other adjusts her skirt. What kind of business did she say she was in?

How do you master body language? How can you learn how to send signals and how to read them? One way is to watch yourself in the mirror. Practice doing a speech or presentation and watch what you do with your hands, feet or eyebrows. Ask a friend or family member if there are specific habits or gestures they've noticed you do when you are engaged in conversation or when you don't know you're being watched. Most of us have some signature gesture or habit that others notice that we may not even be aware of. Some typical gestures and their interpretations are:

- **Crossed arms:** Arms crossed over the chest sometimes suggest that a person is not open to the subject or ideas that are being discussed. It might be interpreted that they are closed-minded or angry.

- **Furrowed brow:** Some people furrow their brow when they are deep in thought or reading or straining to see something. Often people misconstrue this gesture to mean that the person with the furrowed brow is angry, worried or confused.

- **Yawning or stretching:** This gesture typically means that someone is tired or physically uncomfortable but you can often be interpreted as boredom, disinterest or impatience.

- **Foot or finger tapping:** Some people have the habit of unconsciously tapping their foot, fingers or pencil. Some even shake their knee so that their chair or table moves. Usually these are energetic people who can't help but move constantly, but people in their company find the habit unnerving or distracting and often think these people are uninterested in the topic at hand.

- **Fidgeting or playing with hair, chin or neck:** People usually do these things when they are nervous and their lack of self-confidence will be obvious to everyone in the room.

- **Nodding:** In lieu of saying yes or no, some people nod rapidly or persistently. Often nodding is merely a way of letting others know that they have your attention. To the listener, however, repetitive nodding can be interpreted as dismissive, or even worse, may be taken as agreement or nonverbal consent.

Understanding your personal habits and nonverbal communication gestures will enable you to practice controlling them. This control will benefit you greatly in situations where the balance of power is vital.

Now that you know the value of first impressions, take a moment to do the following quiz.

 Rank the following in order of importance when you are making a judgment based on a first meeting. Then rank your own skills in each area in order of your strongest attribute to weakest.

Strongest		Weakest
	Clean & neat appearance	
	Handshake	
	Friendly smile	
	Posture	
	Appropriate clothing	
	Expressions	
	Speech styles	
	General mood	
	Smell/fragrance	
	Tact/self-control	
	Listening skills	
	Knowledge/preparation	
	Sense of humor	
	Consideration/politeness	
	Respect for time	
	Tone of voice	

(See answers at the end of this chapter.)

G. Chapter summary

Points to remember: Good manners are an investment in yourself and in your company. You have a maximum of 60 seconds to make a first impression so make it count. When you meet someone, stand, make eye contact, shake his or her hand, smile and say hello.   Be mindful of the message you send through your body language. Most communication is seen and not heard.

ANSWERS TO SELF-ASSESSMENT QUIZ

1. True: You should wear the nametag on the right because the majority of people shake right-handed. As a handshaker reaches to shake your hand, his/her eyes will automatically glance at your nametag. Further, the left side is traditionally reserved for badges of honor, ribbons or jewelry with emotional meaning, or corsages.

2. False: Whoever is designated the host, or whoever is the highest in "rank" should initiate a handshake. If this person is unaware that this is his or her responsibility and the handshake never comes, anyone may instigate just as long as someone does.

3. False: A formal event dictates that a dress jacket and tie are required.

4. False: The handshake should end after two or three pumps from the elbow, however, the smile and eye contact should continue until the introduction is complete.

5. True: Standing when you meet someone is a way of communicating that you respect him/her,

recognize his/her status and are interested in the introduction. If you are seated at a table or desk, you should rise and come out from behind the desk to greet people.

6. False: Gossip is the height of incivility in the workplace. Refrain from participating whenever possible.

7. False: The correct way to introduce someone is to say the name of the person of higher status first. In a business situation, the boss is more important than a spouse.

8. True: If you associate a person's name with an unrelated object, you will probably remember the name better. For example, if I meet a woman named Mrs. Bunne, I might visualize her holding a rabbit. Next time I see her, the image of the rabbit should come to mind and I will recall that her name is Bunne.

9. True: You have a very narrow window of opportunity to make a first impression. Make it count.

10. False: In business, men should do for women associates the same things they would do for men. If the man would not hang the coat or pull out the chair for a male junior executive, he

should not do so for a female junior executive either and the woman should not expect it. If however, a businessman behaves chivalrously in a business situation, a woman should graciously accept.

ANSWERS TO FIRST IMPRESSIONS QUIZ

There is no sure-fire right or wrong answers; however, research suggests that in most North American business contexts, your tone of voice, posture, and eye contact say a lot about your confidence and credibility. Additionally, how people judge the appropriateness of your physical dress and demeanor based on a specific setting, can help build impressions of competence. One important issue is understanding that if you judge others based on certain elements in a first impression- you should be sure that you have addressed those elements yourself, this helps build trust.

CHAPTER 2

LET ME INTRODUCE MYSELF:

Introduction Guidelines

Now that you've approached, or been approached by, someone and the preliminaries have been taken care of, how do you proceed with the introductions? This can become a very complicated process. The most important thing to keep in mind is that any introduction is better than no introduction. In addition, a polite person is not going to pint out the error of your ways. The only exception would be if you have mispronounced a name or incorrectly attached a title or label.

> Etiquette dictates that if introduction errors occur, they should be corrected promptly. This saves all parties involved from potential further embarrassment. For example, if you name is Miss Braun and you are addressed as Mrs. Brown, you should make the correction immediately.

Remember etiquette is about putting others at ease and handling an awkward situation with dignity. If you found yourself in an awkward situation, which involved introductions, would you know what to do? Take the self-assessment and find out.

Regardless of any other rules, the most important thing to remember about introductions is-MAKE THEM. If you are unsure of the "rules" or the proper order to introduce someone, don't worry about it and do the best you can. It is far ruder not to make an introduction that it is to introduce in the wrong order. Chances are the people you are meeting are also unsure and even if they do know better, they should be polite enough not to say anything.

QUIZ: SELF-ASSESSMENT

1. If you are being introduced to a person with no hands, what would you do

    a. Shake his/her shoulder
    b. Wait for his/her to indicate how the greeting will proceed
    c. Pat him/her on the shoulder

2. The first time you meet a client, she skips the handshake and hugs you close, what do you do?

    a. Hug her back
    b. Pull away slightly and grip her arm to indicate you are uncomfortable

    c. Make a joke butt get the point across that you are surprised by the greeting

3. You meet someone who has a lazy eye, where do you look?

    a. At the area between his/her eyes
    b. Don't look at his/her eyes at all
    c. Choose one eye and maintain contact

4. How would you introduce your boss to your spouse?

    a. Mr. Boss, I'd like you to meet my husband_____
    b. Husband, this is my boss, Mr. Boss
    c. Husband, I'd like to introduce Mr. Boss

5. What do you do if you forget someone's name when you are being introduced?

    a. Fake it and avoid having to say the person's name
    b. Apologize and ask the person what his/her name is
    c. Excuse yourself and rush away

6. How do you react when you approach a group and no one extends their hand or attempts an introduction?

    a. Extend your hand and introduce yourself

    b. Ask if you may join the group and just start talking

    c. Interrupt them and pass out your business card

7. What do you do when you are introduced to a visually impaired person?

    a. Talk louder than usual

    b. Wait for him/her to extend their hand and proceed as usual

    c. Stand close to him/her and talk about yourself

8. If a colleague of yours joins your table, are you obligated to introduce them to everyone at the table?

    a. No, you just need to say hello and speak to them yourself

    b. No, this is up to the host to do

    c. Yes, even if you do not know everyone at the table.

9. How would you introduce yourself to a dignitary?

    a. You wouldn't. Wait for them to introduce themselves to you

    b. Ask the host at the event to introduce you

    c. Just approach them and extend your hand

10. How do you greet yourself to someone when there is a language barrier?

    a. Don't bother, you're wasting your time

    b. Just proceed as normal, only speak slower and louder

    c. Make eye contact, smile and extend your hand. No speech is necessary to make someone feel welcome

A. The status quo

The chart below outlines the direction of introductions. Remember in business situations the client is always the most important person and in social situations the non-business person is always the most important person.

Greater Status	Lesser Status
Client	Anyone
Your boss	Junior executive

Old colleague	New colleague
Guest of honor	Anyone
President	Significant other
Significant other	Acquaintance

If, for example you are at your staff Christmas party and you wish to introduce your boss to your spouse, you would say, "Mr. Boss, I'd like you to meet my husband, Mr. Wonderful." If, however, your husband and you run into your boss at the neighborhood grocery store, you would say, "Mr. Wonderful, I'd like you to meet my boss. Mr. Boss this is my husband." In whichever situation, business or social, the person of lower rank is "presented" to the person of higher rank. The person who is more accomplished in the particular situation "receives" the person less accomplished. One easy way to get it straight is to always say the highest-ranking person's name first.

It's always a good idea to mention the person's title if you know it, and/or say something about the person you are introducing. This provides a starting place for them to have a conversation. For example, when introducing y our boss to a new client you might say, "Mr. Client, I'd like to introduce you to my boss the CEO of XYZ Company. Mr. Boss, this is Mr. Client; he is the marketing manager for STV Company who is just coming on board with us. You may remember meeting him/her at the client appreciation party last week." This saves both the boss and the client the embarrassment of not remembering each other's name, title or forgetting where they met. In addition, each may show the appropriate respect to the other. In theory, the boss should extend his hand to the new client, but it doesn't really matter as long as someone initiates a handshake.

If you are introducing more than one person at a time, try to introduce them according to their rank. If you are unsure of everyone's names or rank, simply say, "Ladies and gentlemen, I'd like you all to meet Mr. Guest of Honor." This is an unspoken directive for everyone to extend their hands and introduce themselves. If no one takes the bait, prompt them further by saying to one person who you do know, "Mr. Save Me Please, I'll let you start the introductions."

B. You know, what's his name? Tips on remembering names

What if you forget someone's name when you are being introduced? Here are some tips on remembering names. Whatever you do, don't try to fake it-you'll only end up looking silly.

- Repeat name during introduction
- Repeat name when departing
- Associate name with object or situation
- Associate name with someone you know personally

TIP: Wear your nametag on the right side. Most people are right-handed and when they reach to shake your hand their eye will automatically go to your nametag. Seeing your name written will help them remember it.

QUIZ: INTRODUCTION SCENARIOS

Now that you know some of the guidelines for introductions, how would you handle yourself in the scenarios outline here?

1. You are one of several guests at a formal dinner. You have been seated with four people you've never met before. What would you say or do?

2. You have a c-worker who is constantly hanging around your office, eavesdropping on your telephone conversations, gossiping and generally wasting your time. What would you do?

3. In the middle of a conversation with a potential client, your associate tells an off-color joke. It is obvious that the client is uncomfortable. What would you do?

4. At the annual Christmas party you are designated the hostess. How would you introduce the following?

    a. Your boss to your key client
    b. Your co-worker to your spouse
    c. One client to another
    d. Your receptionist to a higher-up

5. You are in the middle of a meeting with a
    client in your office. Your phone rings and
    the call display indicates that it's your boss.
    What would you do?

    (See answers at the end of this chapter.)

C. Let the games begin: Proper use of business cards

We can thank our Japanese friends for the ritual of
business cards. The exchange of business cards is
one of the most important communication behaviors
in business and it is practiced all over the world.
Make sure you have cards with you wherever you go
and remember the following rules:

- **How to give your card:** You should present
  your card as if it is a gift you are giving
  someone. Be discriminate and don't become
  known as "The Collector" or "The Blackjack
  Dealer."   When you are giving your card,
  "present" it with the writing away from you
  so the receiver can take a moment to read it
  and ask questions. Make sure your card is
  clean and not scribbled on or bent.   The

business card is a mini-snapshot of you professionally and it will be a factor in people's first impression of you.

- **When to give your card:** You should offer your card if you are involved in a conversation and the other party has expressed interest in you or what you do. Do not give out cards in social situations. Soliciting business at public events like weddings, funerals, and house parties is considered in very poor taste.

- **Asking for someone else's card:** If you are a subordinate, you should wait until a superior offers you a card. Similarly, do not ask for business cards in social situations and be discreet in business when you ask. Remember, the potential client or potential employer is handing you a gift when they give their card and there are responsibilities that go along with accepting the gift.

- **Business cards as part of correspondence:** Only give business cards when business is involved. For example, it would not be appropriate to attach a business card when you send flowers to a co-worker or client who has had a death in the family. Nor would it be appropriate to attach a business card to a fit sent to someone when they've just had a baby. An easy rule to remember is that if there is emotion involved (do not send a business card). In theory, our emotions should not be mixed up with our business, right? Incidentally this is also the guideline when deciding whether to personalize (handwrite) a letter/note or not.

When giving or receiving business cards, try to avoid the examples of these characters:

THE COLLECTOR: This indiscreet individual collects cards as if they were collector's item baseball cards. They pick up cards everywhere they go and are sometimes very obvious about how their filing system works. Left jacket pocket-Keepers, Right pants pocket-discards, inside pocket-Use for scrap paper or toothpicks.

THE BLACKJACK DEALER: This person doles out cards like it's a poker game. People will have a tendency to think the card is less valuable if everyone has one. It's a strange phenomenon, sort of like people will wait longer to get into a busy nightclub if there's already a line forming when they arrive. The harder things are to get, the more people want them.

D. But is it art? The lost art of conversation

Apparently in days of old, conversation was an art. Much emphasis was placed on grammar, vocabulary, and tone of voice. People even hand-wrote letters to each other regularly. A feather pen was the vessel for poetry in motion. There's no question that people in general have forgotten their manners when it comes to conversation. People will talk about anything. The chart below lists some appropriate and inappropriate topics for conversation. Remember, how you feel, or your opinion, is secondary in business conversations. The only thing you should be concerned about is making the client feel comfortable.

It's all about the investment of time and you'd hate to lose a deal because you've insulted someone during a casual conversation. Remember, the best conversationalist is a good listener.

Inappropriate topics regardless of the social or business situation are:

Divorce, sickness, personal issues: Meet SHERRY SPRING IT ON ME. No topic is off limits for Sherry. Whether it's her grandma's hemorrhoids, her last boyfriend's prowess or the details of her last divorce... She will spring it on you when you least expect it.

- **Grapefruit, fiber, protein or any other diet:** RICKY SLIMMONS and his opinions on eating are a continual headache during any luncheon meeting. Prepare to swallow a fair portion of guilt if eating just one French fry in front of this calorie counter. Keep your dieting tips to yourself Ricky; we would all rather enjoy our meals.

- **Touchy topics:** Anything about which another party has strong convictions is a touchy topic. If it's rude, demeaning, lewd, racist, or prejudiced, ARCHIE BUNGLER will say it and he doesn't care whose listening. Wide eyes, gasps of disbelief and disgruntled guests just encourage him. There is nothing Archie likes better than a bantering session about a hot topic he knows very little about. He'll make it up as he goes along though and argue until he's the only blue-faced Bunker in the room.

- **Yourself:** Meet IVANA TALKALOT with whom conversations might sound like this, "Oh hello, it's nice to meet you. Let me tell you all about myself and how much I paid for this dress. You're quite lucky I came along when I did or you'd have missed out on hearing all about me. Don't bother telling me about you and I won't ask because I'm really more interesting and Ivana Talkalot about myself. Unless, that is... you're willing to divulge the price of your new summer home".

- **Just because you think something is funny does not mean others will:** Witness -THE STAND UP COMIC who is always performing- "I'm the funniest person you'll ever meet; I even crack myself up which you probably noticed by my extra loud laughter. If you don't laugh at my jokes the first time I'll repeat them over and over until you do. And wait until I'm drunk. That's when the practical jokes come out; remember when I snuck that dribble cup into the management meeting. Ha! Ha! Ha!"

Appropriate topics for any social or business situation are:

- Good news
- Congratulations
- Weddings, births and celebrations
- Cultural events
- Sporting events
- Web sites
- Books, movies, magazines

- Weather

There are probably additional inappropriate topics that apply to your specific line of business.

E. Is anybody listening?

Speech style is what differentiates us when it comes to public speaking and presenting ourselves conversationally. Mastery of appropriate speech style enables you to present your case in a way that encourages others to listen. Polished speech style incorporates the following:

Speech styles include:

- **Tone of voice:** Your tone should be even but not monotonous or without expression. Depending on the speaker's style, the tone of voice can make the message formal or informal, instructional or preachy and so on. Tone of voice is often indicative of the speaker's mood or attitude. A slow, lifeless tone of voice can be as frustrating as a high-pitched, squeaky voice. Tape record yourself and see how you sound to others.

- **Volume:** When you speak, the volume should be just loud enough that listeners do not have to strain to hear but quiet enough that they have to focus to get the point you're making.

- **Gestures:** Remember that your nonverbal communication is a sub-text to your verbal communication. Make sure you are in control of the messages you're sending. Dramatic hand, arm or facial gestures are often more distracting than informative.

- **Accommodation:** Make sure your message is being delivered at a level you audience can comprehend. Conversation, including vocabulary and tone, should be adjusted depending on whom you are speaking with. It goes without saying that you would speak differently to a group of school children than you would a board of directors.

- **Listening:** Pause on occasion and listen for feedback-verbal or otherwise, from the audience.

- **Embellishment:** Everyone loves a good story. Just be sure that you're believable. If you do have your audience's full attention, someone in the crowd is bound to call you on the facts.

F. Chapter summary

Here are the key things to consider when it comes to the art of conversation:

- Limit personal conversation during business hours
- Avoid name dropping and gossip
- Do not ask personal questions
- Speak clearly and use proper grammar
- Remember that conversations are rarely kept in confidence

ANSWERS TO SELF-ASSESSMENT QUIZ

1. b) Stand, smile and make eye contact but wait until the person indicates how he/she wishes to proceed with the introduction.

2. c) Without making the client uncomfortable you can use your sense of humor to get the message across that you are uncomfortable with the hugging. When you meet next, put your hand out immediately to show you prefer to shake hands.

3. a) Look at the area between his/her eyes. The person knows you are unsure where to look and may say something to let you know he/she is comfortable with the situation.

4. a) In a business situation, you would say Mr. Boss, I'd like you to meet my husband Bob.

5. b) You should look him/her in the eye, apologize and ask them to repeat his/her name. A sincere smile and sense of humor will also help.

6. a) If no one is taking the initiative, you should go ahead and start the introduction process

7. b) Wait for the person to verbalize a greeting or extend his/her hand. Do not touch the

person unless he/she gestures that it is okay to do so.

8. a) If you know the other people at the table, it would be nice to introduce everyone, however, you need only introduce yourself and let the newcomer proceed at his/her own level of comfort.

9. b) Answer a) would be fine too but the best choice is to ask the event host to introduce you.

10. c) A sincere smile and eye contact is often enough to make someone feel comfortable when there is a language barrier, without drawing attention to the issue. A handshake reinforces respect. There is no need to struggle with words.

ANSWERS TO INTRODUCTION SCENARIOS

1. If you are seated with people you have never met and the host who seats you did not make introductions, you should stand and introduce yourself to those at the table. As newcomers join, rise and introduce yourself to them as well.

2. If you have a bothersome co-worker, the easiest thing to do is shut your door and lock it if possible when you are taking important calls or handling clients. You could also speak directly to the person and express your concerns with a sense of humor.   If this doesn't work, bring it up with your supervisor.

3. The best way to handle this situation is to somehow let the client know that you do not approve of the joke either, but to do so without embarrassing the associate who told it. Alternatively, you could change the subject, say, "I'm not sure that's funny" or just ignore it. Eye contact with the client will be most important and make a point of apologizing to the client when alone. Let your associate know in private that his/her actions were inappropriate.

4. a) Mr. Client, I'd like to introduce my boss, Mr. Blank. The client is always the most important person in business.

    b) Mr. Co-worker, this is my wife, Mrs. Blank. In business situations, the co-worker's name should be said first. In social situations, for example if you meet a co-worker at the grocery store, the spouse would be the more important person.

    c) Mr. Client who I've worked with longer, I'd like to introduce Mr. New Client. Old relationships take precedence over new relationships when the persons involved are of the same "rank".

    d) Mr. Higher-Up, I'd like you to meet our receptionist Anne Brown. In North American business, gender is irrelevant; the only thing that counts is rank.

5. Let the phone ring. In business the client is always the most important person. I'm sure your boss will be glad that you understand this concept. Also, in every situation, the person who is present should be treated as more important than the person who is not. For example, my dinner partner should be

more important than the person who might be calling my cell phone.

CHAPTER 3

INTEROFFICE COMMUNICATION:
Someone's been sitting in my chair...

Work is not what it used to be. Modern workplaces offer fast-paced and complicated interaction in new and unfamiliar social and business situations. Along with dramatic advances in technology, such as the cell phone and the Internet, the convenience of home offices, job sharing and the growing number of "young presidents," there has been an incredible gender shift in the office-women are often the bosses and make up half of the workforce. All of this change has made the office a potentially scary quagmire.

So how do we deal with bosses, co-workers, and employees, when we're not quite sure what the rules are? When it comes to office etiquette, the basic rules still apply. Etiquette is about putting others at ease. So when you are dealing with phone and email, you use the same basic techniques you would in person. Whether you are dealing with a male or female co-worker, remember that person is a co-worker first and the same rules apply to both. And when you are dealing with a boss or an employee, there is clear hierarchy that always puts the client first.

How do you rate in the office etiquette scheme of things? Take the self-assessment and see how you fit into the office.

SELF-ASSESSMENT: OFFICE COMMUNICATIONS

	True	False
1. At the office all men and women are created equal. Gender should not be a factor.		
2. When a man shakes a woman's hand he should be less firm than when he shakes a man's hand.		
3. During office hours it is appropriate to address all co-workers, regardless of their rank, by their given name.		
4. If a businessman and a businesswoman are dining		

together, the man should always offer to get the cheque.		
5. When you voicemail co-workers located in the same building, it is not necessary to leave your name, as they'll know your voice.		
6. Women tend to be outwardly affectionate so it's okay for them to hug each other when they greet.		
7. We spend a lot of time with our co-workers so it's all right to discuss personal issues during office hours.		
8. If I feel like butting loose on Friday happy hours at the office, co-workers shouldn't complain because it's after hours.		

9. If I am uncomfortable with a "too-personal" relationship that is going on between two co-workers, I have a responsibility to discuss this with my supervisor.		
10. If everyone in my office chips in to buy gifts for co-workers and I just don't feel it's necessary, I do not have to donate.		

(See answers at the end of this chapter.)

A. Who's the boss?

When it comes to dealing with the boss, three simple rules apply:

- **Listen:** This shows respect and lets the boss know that you know who is in charge. Listen first, give your full attention, and then ask intelligent questions.

- **Be prepared:** This means don't be late, *ever*, and be prepared for anything. Most bosses prefer working with people who are solution-oriented. They generally don't want to know every detail and they certainly don't want to be bothered with your troubles, unless, you're in over your head.

- **Maintain your integrity:** Don't pretend you know something you don't. Don't take credit for things you didn't do-good or bad-and don't be a "brown noser."

THE BROWN NOSER: The brown noser is the worst. "Yes sir, yes sir, how high did you say sir?" Brown nosers are very annoying company to keep. Even more annoying...it's so obvious to everyone else in the office that Brown Nosers are brown-nosing but they come out smelling like a rose anyway.

THE IDOL WORSHIPPER: The idol worshipper is that gung ho, maybe a little naïve employee, who puts the boss or even a co-worker on a pedestal. You can only imagine the disbelief and disappointment when the subject fails to live up to the worshipper's expectations. The unknowing worshipper will never be the same again.

Don't ever forget that although superior in rank, the boss is still "just a regular person" at the end of the day. One of the primary reasons miscommunications occur between employees and the boss is because people have unreasonable expectations when it comes to their superiors. Don't make this mistake. And, don't forget that in business situations, the client is always the most important person. Most bosses would agree, however, you should always make a point of stating your boss's formal title when introducing them to anyone, whether it's a business associate, a social acquaintance or a client.

What do you do when you find yourself in an awkward situation where a co-worker, associate or even your boss is overly familiar or maybe gets too personal when it comes to initial contact or introductions?   Well, for starters, put as much physical distance between you and the person behaving in a too familiar way as possible. Sometimes you can actually control the interaction by saying things like, "Oh, don't get up, we're just passing through, I just wanted to introduce Mr. Client and we'll be on our way." The "close talker" with bad breath, the "groper" or the "chatty" person will not have an opportunity to get too close to the client or associate. If you smile and show that you respect the person's position but maintain control of his or her proximity to the newcomer, you can avoid a potentially uncomfortable situation without offending anyone.

B. Getting along with co-workers

Relationships with peers and co-workers can be the most complicated.   Trust and mutual respect underlie good co-worker relations and it only takes one bad apple to turn the office dynamic rotten. Over the course of daily work life we interact with a wide range of personalities.

> The etiquette crisis on the job not only includes phone slamming, snippy e-mails, yelling, and harsh reprimands, but there's no surprise to learn that "Pet peeve number one among many employees is when people take someone else's food from the refrigerator" (Dr. P.M. Forni, Civility Project, Johns Hopkins University)

The following is a list of rules that can help you get along with co-workers and clients. These are based on the "top ten" rude office behaviors identified by the hundreds of business people we have spoken to in the course of our corporate conduct training sessions.

Top Ten Rules for getting along at the office:

1. **Acknowledge people:**   There is nothing ruder than having lunch with a co-worker or client and then averting your eyes when you pass in the hall or acting as though you've never met when seated across the table for a business meeting.   At minimum, proper etiquette dictates that you acknowledge someone's presence.

2. **Don't gossip:**   Gossip is the height of incivility in the workplace and it is extremely bad manners to assume everyone else is interested in the often spiteful and meaningless tidbits you're passing on. Gossiping does not build trusting work relationships.

3. **Dress properly:**   Inappropriate attire, too short, too tight, too revealing, and too often slept in, etc. It is disrespectful to others and to yourself when productivity or the quality of work is demeaned by distractions resulting from someone's attire. A good rule of thumb is to dress as if you were interviewing for a job everyday. This means that even if "casual" attire is acceptable at work, have a suit jacket or tie or toe-in shoes etc available (in your office or in your car) so that you can take it up a notch at a moments notice and you will be prepared for any situation that could arise on the job, e.g., an impromptu meeting with the boss or a key client, picking a guest/client up at the airport etc.

4. **Don't smoke:** Don't smoke in public places, especially work, except in designated areas. If possible don't smoke at all when with clients.

5. **Hands off the hold button:** Do not put a caller on hold so you can answer your "call waiting." Do not keep people on hold for any reason for extended periods and do return telephone calls within 4 hours if possible. If you're leaving a message, make sure you leave your name and number and a brief message. Nothing is more frustrating than a voicemail message where someone forgets to leave his or her name or number.

6. **Get the name right:** Do not address your supervisor or co-workers by his/her first name or nickname when introducing a client. Always introduce the less accomplished person to the more accomplished person. An easy way to remember proper introduction protocol is to use the most important person's name first. In any case, any introduction is better than no introduction.

7. **Be punctual:** Do not be late and do not keep others waiting. Nothing says, "My time is

worth more than yours" than being late. Too early is not always appropriate either.

8. **Don't interrupt:** Don't drop by just to chat. Interruptions are not always welcome. If the door is shut, knock first. Do not sit down in someone's office until you are invited to do so and if at all possible. Call ahead to make an appointment. Be prepared and stick to the point of the meeting.

9. **Dress at home:**   Your desk is not your bathroom vanity. Do not brush your hair, change your socks, apply make-up or use a toothpick anywhere except the bathroom unless the office door is locked and the blinds are drawn.   Keep your personal hygiene habits private.

10. **Neither a borrower…:** Do return borrowed objects and do not "borrow" anything without permission. This applies to office supplies, reports, ideas, and even clients.

Knowing when and how to separate personal and business matters is at the heart of good business etiquette.   Sometimes, in maintaining good professional relationships, we find ourselves caught up in tricky personal areas. Once again, respect, sincerity, and tact are the keys to successful (and polite) workplace relationships. Confidence and trust are vital to building long term business relationships and it's sometimes impossible to get to know clients well and build trust without exchanging personal details. This is especially difficult these days as we find ourselves in more and more situations where business and pleasure mix. If at all possible, keep personal involvements to a minimum. Once you are mired in someone's personal details, it is very difficult to extricate yourself. Things can get really complicated for example, if you are at a social function unrelated to business and witness a client become intoxicated and behave badly. Even if the client is in the wrong, you may find yourself having to defend his bad behavior for the sake of your business relationship even though you risk your personal and professional reputation.

 Good manners dictate that we not point out character flaws in others, but it is important to recognize annoying behaviors so that we catch ourselves when our own actions are less than exemplary. Etiquettely speaking, what is the proper way to deal with the barrage of Ill-mannered co-workers or clients we encounter? Well, that depends! It depends on three things: how intolerable was the behavior; what is your responsibility towards the person portraying the behavior, and, how valuable/necessary is the client/co-worker/associate?

If the behavior was very intolerable and you have a responsibility to the person who committed the faux pas or if the person is an important team member or client, you will want to handle the situation carefully. At the opportune time where you will not draw additional attention to the action or embarrass the culprit, let him/her know where he/she went wrong. If the error was small and did not have a huge repercussion, let it go. Remember, it's very rude to point out rude behavior. If you cannot afford to offend the person, do nothing, but try to lead by setting a positive example and mend fences after the fact if you can. For example, if a co-worker makes an insensitive or inappropriate remark in front of a client, you may opt to do nothing at the time, however speak to the co-worker about it later in private and do make appropriate apologies to the client. Some behaviors, like lying or stealing are certainly intolerable. Usually company policy and personal ethics dictate behavior in such instances. Finally, if you are responsible for the person who made a manners error, for example you are his/her immediate supervisor, you have a responsibility to make them aware of his/her behavior in a polite but firm manner and set him/her on the path to proper business behaviors.

In daily workplace interactions, we come across a wide variety of personalities. Some will exhibit behaviors that drive you crazy. In every business situation it is important to remember that what is best for business should dictate what behavior is acceptable.

THE FENCE SITTER: This person couldn't make up his/her mind to save his/her life. Every little decision takes much contemplation. The Fence Sitter asks a million inane questions and even with all the information still ends up where he/she started by asking, I don't know, what do you think? Uggggg! No wonder nothing ever gets done around here.

THE PRAISE MONGER: This is the co-worker who rarely contributes to the task at hand but miraculously appears when the work is done and the accolades are being handed out. Suddenly he/she is an expert on the project and is more than happy to take ownership for the work. The praise monger disappears in a flash, however, if the reviews are less than positive.

CAPTAIN DOOM AND GLOOM: If you've never met someone this negative, you've been lucky. A big, black cloud follows Captain Doom and Gloom. The first words out of his mouth are usually "no" or "I can't." Pessimist through and through! Even when things are going great, Captain Gloomy can find something to complain about.

C. How to treat your employees

Showing others respect is the best way to earn respect. This is the golden rule for interacting with employees. Employees demand less time, attention and money if they know they have the respect of their superiors. They won't feel taken advantage of, they'll communicate their needs better, and there will be a mutual trust between employee and employer.

As the captain of the ship, the diverse needs of your crew can sometimes make one feel like jumping ship. Here are a few life preservers to help you swim, not sink. Your crew will appreciate your insight and versatility when dealing with their needs.

- **You're simply the best, better than all the rest!** Some employees need a lot of praise in order to work at their best. But the difficulty with constant encouragement is that it can become exhausting and insincere. Schedule a weekly 20 minute meeting with this employee to set goals and respond to the previous week's attained goals.   Be supportive and encouraging but keep meetings short and sweet. Respect for this person will benefit your company as he/she will work hard for your encouragement and will remain loyal workers.

- **You're not the boss of me:** There are always a few people on the work team who were directing the kids in the sandbox at day care on proper sandcastle structuring. As a team member the resentment they can cause among their peer group can be detrimental to your company. Although these employees can usually accomplish more in a day than most of us can in a week, the "Bossy Bob or Betsy" needs to curtail their demanding ways. As part of your discussion with them, they need to understand that final decisions are not always theirs. In their job description, the parameters of their responsibilities must be extremely detailed. They will respond to positive feedback and constructive criticism more readily than censure. Be polite yet firm with discipline.

- **The over-achiever:** This bundle of energy has a knack for finishing a project before the rest of the company can get to the drawing board. Keeping over-achievers challenged can become a challenge. They can be counted on to perform but if boredom sets in the over-achiever may become an under-the-table nuisance. Keep a list of duties that need to be completed and request a proposal from this employee for potential projects he/she would suggest as important for company growth.

As the leader of a team of individuals the constant change in your office can become tiring and at times annoying. A great guide must lead by example and remember that employees are judging and mirroring simultaneously. Be respectful of your team as individuals not only as a unit. Respect team members' differences and celebrate their achievements. If a leader exhibits polite behavior and respectful responses the company policies will revolve around that positive culture.

Many managers believe that success and power equal respect. All of us, I am sure, have been lucky enough to be led down the beaten path (with beaten brows) by Attila the Hun who believes that if people cringe in fear when they enter a room they are being shown respect. Hah! There is a distinct difference between following out of fear and following out of respect. Employees who know that the chopping block has a permanent place in their office are rarely productive long-term. Management by intimidation went the way of the pet rock and mood ring. In the new millennium good manners and respect for others equals success and smooth sailing.

D. The gossip mill...churning and churning

Gossip is the height of incivility in the workplace, and in spite of this, it is the most common etiquette issue in the workplace. We are all wise to remember that chances are, if you are talking about someone, he/she is talking about you too. The best way to handle awkward or uncomfortable gossip moments is to let others know you are not interested in gossip. By not responding or changing the subject others will quickly understand that you have no interest in the topic of discussion. If you do not make comments about others tales but are still quick to repeat them, this behaviour will quickly catch up with you and before you know it you will become the next target. Sometimes just politely nodding and excusing yourself from gossip-driven situations is the easiest and best approach.

If you find that others in your workplace continually comment on other office employees, respond by defending the gossip victim(s). Sometimes positivity is contagious. Try politely disagreeing with the negative comments, for example, "Oh really, the report was on my desk far before the deadline" or "I always find her/him friendly and accommodating." Gossipers will find you boring and move on to another target.   Or, the best case scenario is that you can change the whole tone of the office by watching as others mirror your professional response.   If you hear gossip about yourself and know that it is not true you have a couple of choices.   A) Start a rumor with the queen/king of the gossip mill about yourself that will make others laugh and realize you cannot be intimidated, or B) ignore it, and hope the gossip mongers move on to someone else. As a last alternative, C) you can confront the gossipers, or address the gossip head on and tell your group at the next meeting, in a clever manner, the real circumstance or how something really happened.

If you hear something about a major shake up in your company let your director know what you have heard.   You do not need to tell him/her who, what and where, just the information.   Let the Director know that you are not fishing for an answer just that you thought he/she might like to know about this major disruption.   Usually, leadership will appreciate your honesty and your information may give them a chance to end gossip that might get out of hand.

The difference between a gossiper and someone who tells plenty of stories or has lots to say is the context in which a story is told and sometimes the intention with which it is told. Keep your stories about others friendly and positive. If stories are nasty or malicious keep them to yourself.

Please meet our office celebrities who sometimes sink before they swim (If you don't drown them first).

CHATTY CATHY: If there's a story in there somewhere Cathy is going to find it and repeat it. Typically Cathy is known for gossiping and is often called by other not so flattering names. If you want to know something, ask Cathy. If she's not sure she'll make something up.

THE PSYCHIC: The office psychic knows what is happening before you do. It's unclear where he/she gets his/her information. The psychic is often incorrect but his/her speculation is enough to get the office news wheel moving. Here's a prediction for the psychic, I bet he/she will be out of a job soon if he/she doesn't start keeping his/her opinions to him/herself.

E. Integrity and ethics at work

When we enter the work environment, we have to remember some of the basic tips for etiquette and personal responsibility that we (hopefully) use in our own lives. If etiquette is about putting others at ease, then integrity and ethics are about governing our own behavior and living up to basic moral codes that are useful both in our personal and our work lives.

There are four factors that are fundamental in maintaining integrity and ethics in the workplace:

- **Accountability:**   This is another word for integrity in business. Say what you mean and mean what you say.   Don't make commitments you cannot keep and answer for your actions.

- **Familiarity:** This concept in business refers to basic respect and issues of confidentiality and trust. We spend a lot of time with co-workers and clients and often find ourselves involved with people on personal as well as professional levels. Whenever possible, keep confidences. If someone lets down their guard and shares something about him/herself with you, treat this as a gift and handle it with respect.

- **Responsibility:** In this sense, responsibility has to do with ethics and is more about our responsibilities or duties with regard to the people we work with, whether clients or co-workers. We have a personal responsibility on a human level to treat these people with consideration, respect and honesty. We have personal responsibilities not to jeopardize the health and safety of people and to represent ourselves to them as we really are. For example, don't lie about past experience, don't deliberately make other's feel bad and don't bait people.

- **Reasonability:** Refers to what is logical and reasonable in a business environment. This goes to the question of ethics. For example, is it reasonable to assume you'll be paid for overtime work if you are not productive during office hours? Is it reasonable to assume that you will not be suspended even if you disregard company policy just because you've been there so long?

How do you rate when it comes to ethics? Let's find out.

SELF-ASSESSMENT: ETHICS

1. What do you do if you hear a rumor that could undermine the boss's authority?

a) Tell your boss
b) Try to find out who's spreading it and stop it
c) Mind your own business and don't repeat it

2.   A co-worker has been discussing confidential client issues over a casual lunch with other associates, what would you do?

a) Change the subject
b) Excuse yourself and ask the co-worker to join you for a moment
c) Interrupt and tell her she's breaking the rules

3. You receive a delivery of office supplies; you notice that there are items present that were not invoiced for, what do you do?

a) Call the supplier and straighten it out

b) Put the items in a storage room and say nothing
c) Hide the articles in your office

4. You happen upon a co-worker's stash of inappropriate magazines, what do you do?

a) Ignore them, it's none of your business
b) Take the magazines and throw them out
c) Report to your boss

5. You are consistently interrupted by a co-worker who insists on dropping by to chat, what do you do?

a) Ask him/her politely not to come by without calling first
b) Shut your door
c) Ignore him/her and keep working

6. A client who was happy with the services you provided sent a very expensive thank you gift to the office, what do you do?

a) Call the client, say you cannot keep the gift and send it back
b) Explain the situation to your supervisor and do as instructed
c) Keep it and send the client a thank you card

7. You've got some sick days and you'd really like to take a long weekend so...

a) Make plans and leave your boss a voicemail message late at night
b) Book the days off in advance as holidays, you never know when you'll be sick for real
c) Check your workload and see if you can arrange for someone else to cover you

8. You pay into the coffee fund every week but you drink far less coffee than most people. What would you do?

a) Bring it up at the next staff meeting and see where it goes
b) Put a note up asking people to limit their coffee intake
c) Do nothing, it's one of those office things you have to live with

9. Even with your office door shut you can clearly hear private conversations coming from the room next door. What should you do?

a) Say nothing and try not to listen
b) Tell the person in the office so that he/she can adjust his/her conversations accordingly
c) Listen and make notes, you never know when the information will come in handy

10. You've intercepted a private email which was intended for a co-worker who no longer works at the office so you...

a) Pass the email along to everyone you know
b) Contact the sender and let him/her know what's happened
c) Delete the message and never mention it

(See answers at the end of this chapter.)

F. Gender relations in the business arena

Unlike social etiquette, which in theory is based on gender and chivalry, business etiquette is often based on hierarchy and power. Gender should not play a significant role. Every man and woman should be treated equally well. Some important things to remember:

- The most important person in any company or in any business dealings is the client or customer

- Persons of lesser importance (Business-wise) or accomplishment are presented to persons of greater importance, regardless of gender. The name of the least important person is said last.   The "greater" with respect to business is presented to the "lesser."

- Doors are held for persons more senior in rank, regardless of gender. Whoever gets to the door first, and it should be the person with less seniority who holds a door for the others. If it is a revolving door, "lesser" goes first to get the door moving, then waits on the other side for all the "greaters."

- Elevators empty from the front to back regardless of gender.

- Only those who need assistance with chairs should be helped at business functions.

- Both genders should be helped with their coats if they are clients or more senior in rank.

- The general rule for mixed gender meetings for men is that if you would not do something, i.e., stand upon entrance, pull out a chair, kiss on the cheek, comment on appearance, etc. for a male associate, you should not do it for a female associate.

- The general rule for mixed gender meetings for women is that you should not expect men in business to treat you the way they would socially. However, if a man in business does behave "chivalrously," do not act all bothered and defensive. Chances are he means no disrespect.

In any office or business environment we unfortunately come across those who disregard the rules. These are often the employees who have trouble understanding why they are not respected. Please forgive these characters, as life in the office would be extremely dull without them.

THE MASSAGER: It might be a man, it might be a woman, and maybe you've got one of each. The massager can seem like an office worker's best friend. They think they're doing you a favor with the impromptu back rubs but they're not. Unless the boss has arranged an in-house tension relieve program, we'd pass on this one.

THE HONEYMOONERS: Don't open the storage room without knocking. You may find yourself looking in on the honeymooners. Do these two really think their romance is a big secret? Shish! We'll give them three months.

THE KITTEN/TOMCAT: Do you hear purring? This is the guy or gal who thinks every gal or guy in the office wants it, bad, and they're the ones who've got it. You can never be too careful around these two. A friendly smile at the copy machine might get you engaged.

QUIZ: OFFICE SCENARIOS

Here are some scenarios which involve inter-office communications, how would you handle yourself in each one?

1. You've just received an invitation to a client's open house and it's on the same night as another function to which you have already committed. What would you do now?

2. You are hosting an event and several guests have unexpectedly brought along their spouses. What would you do?

3. You are entertaining a client at a local restaurant and the service is deplorable. How would you handle this?

4. At a fancy cocktail reception, you spill red wine all over a guest. What would you do?

5. You have been waiting all day for an important client to return a call you left the day prior. You have to meet a deadline. What would you do?

6. You are in charge of a group of employees and are consistently dismayed at their general appearance. How would you address this?

(See answers at the end of this chapter.)

G. Chapter summary

The "office" has changed dramatically and so have the rules for office conduct. Technology is not an etiquette free zone and, in fact, we need to be more conscious of our behavior in spite of all modern conveniences, which seem to dictate otherwise. With a large population of men and women working together the awareness of gender related etiquette has become vital. There are Ten Commandments for the office, which will help you maintain your integrity and ethics at work:

1. *Thou shalt not lust after a co-worker.*

2. *Thou shalt not put thy superiors on a pedestal.*

3. *Thou shalt not borrow.*

4. *Thou shalt treat all as equals.*

5. *Thou shalt not lie, gossip or tell tall tales.*

6. *Thou shalt not be late.*

7. *Thou shalt not pass the buck.*

8. *Thou shalt not steal.*

9. *Thou shalt clean up after thyself.*

10. *Thou shalt listen.*

Answers to office communications self-assessment

1. True: In business gender is irrelevant. Rank is the only thing that mattes

2. False: Men and women should shake each other's hands with the same professional firm handshake.

3. False: During office hours, higher-ranking persons should be addressed by their surnames, particularly in front of clients. Given (first) names should be reserved for closed business situations.

4. False: In a business situation, whoever did the inviting should get the check.

5. False: Regardless of whom you are calling or where you are calling from, you should always leave your name, time of call and reason for calling.

6. False: Women in business should refrain from familiar touching which includes hugging and kissing.

7. False: Whenever possible, personal issues should stay personal.

8. False: Whenever you are in a business environment with business people you should be on your business behavior. Whenever you mix business and pleasure, you will be judged according.

9. False: Your first responsibility is to the co-worker.   Without embarrassing them, give them an opportunity to revise their behaviors.   If you are consistently placed in awkward situations and they do not seem to respect your feelings, go to your supervisor.

10. False: Etiquette dictates that if you do not want to alienate yourself you need to participate.   You should find some way to broach the issue and find a compromise. Maybe as a group you can set limits on the dollar values.   Chances are others are feeling the same way you are.

Answers to ethics self-assessment

1. c) Mind your own business and don't repeat it

2. a) As politely as you can, change the subject and let the co-worker know you are disappointed in their behavior when you're in private.

3. a) Honesty is most always the best policy.

4. a) Unless you are the supervisor, it's none of your business.

5. b) Shut your door. If that doesn't work talk to them directly.

6. b) Your company may have a policy you don't know about in this regard. Check with your supervisor.

7. b) or c) Although it's tempting to see if you can get away with faking a sick day, don't. People know when you're for real. Maintain our integrity and do the right thing.

8. a) or c) Either bring it up at a meeting and see where it goes, maybe others feel the way you do, or do nothing. Grin and bear it, maybe you use more staples than they do.

9. b) Definitely let the person know the situation.

10. b) Contact the sender and let him/her know what's happened.

Answers to office scenarios

1. If you have already sent an RSVP to one function, you have an obligation to attend. Graciously decline the second invitation. The only exception would be if the events are casual, come and go functions which could both be attended.

2. Happily greet the guests, covertly add some place settings and adjust portions and seating as required. While it is in very bad taste to bring along uninvited guests, it is equally rude to make them feel uncomfortable. For the next party, be very clear with invitations how many persons are invited.

3. Whatever you do, don't cause a scene in front of your client. You should quietly pay the bill,

tip the minimum so you will not be perceived as petty or cheap, take the manager's card and proceed with your meeting. After the client has left, speak with the manager or telephone with your concerns at a later date.

4. Do not touch the person or try to wipe their clothing. Apologize of course and call a service attendant. Offer to take care of the person's cleaning bill, give your business card to show you are sincere and then drop the subject.

5. Call again. If you get the person's voicemail either leave a firm but polite message or speak with the receptionist, explain the situation and have the person paged. Hold a general meeting and outline the office policy. Make sure the employees understand how their professional presence affects the company. Set a standard, lead by example and enforce the guidelines.

CHAPTER 4

TECHNOLOGY:
The new etiquette

In spite of what you might think, technology is not an etiquette-free zone. In general, all of the normal rules of etiquette apply offline, also apply online. For example, if you would not normally say something to someone over the telephone, you certainly should not say it via email where it will be stored for eternity for the entire world to read at will. Three key things to think about when using the Internet: confidentiality, familiarity, and reasonability. An easy rule of thumb is-would I tell this joke, pass on this note, write this card, spend this time or approach this person, in person? If not, chances are it's better left undone on the Internet, email, fax or voicemail as well.

In Book Two of the In Good Company series *P's and Q's for Profit*, we cover office communications and technology in depth, but the following is a quick overview of the basics.

Cell phones typically come with users' manuals but they rarely include etiquette guidelines. How much do you know about etiquette and technology?

Self-assessment

1. If someone emails you asking you not to send them any more unsolicited "span," they are referring to:

a) Junk mail in the form of email advertising or chain letters etc.
b) An email which was accidentally sent to the wrong address
c) Copies of email which was previously sent

2. A co-worker has had a death in the family. You want to send condolences. What would you do?

a) Send an email
b) Mail a handwritten note
c) Pass a card around the office and leave it on his/her desk

3. You're waiting for a client to close on a big deal. He/she said they'd call by 4:00 and it's ten after five. You should:

a) Call immediately and find out what's going on
b) Give him/her the benefit of the doubt and wait until he/she calls

c) Email him/her and leave your home number

4. You don't have an email at home so your friends often email personal messages at work. Sometimes the messages are really personal. How would you handle this?

a) Email back, it's your private email and it's no one's business
b) Quickly put a stop to all personal emails sent to work. Telephone friends and family from the privacy of your own home
c) Just don't return the email

5. Your cell phone rings in the middle of an important staff meeting. What should you do?

a) Answer it, it's a business call
b) Say excuse me and quietly leave the room to take the call
c) Immediately shut the phone off and apologize to the group

6. You're fed up with the behavior and attitude of a co-worker. You correspond regularly by email and you want to say your piece so...

a) Email your comments to the co-worker and cc your boss
b) Call the co-worker on the phone and ask to meet in person to discuss the issues

c) Write your feelings down and say nothing. Come back to the issue when you're calm

7. You're sitting in a restaurant and you cannot help over hearing a cell phone conversation a competitor is having in the booth next to you. Good manners dictate that you...

a) Listen, he/she is a fool with bad manners
b) Ignore him/her and try not to listen
c) Interrupt him/her and let them know you are present and can overhear the conversation

8. You collected a handful of business cards at a business cocktail party and want to contact one of the people you met and spoke to briefly. It is appropriate to:

a) Email him/her and strike up a conversation
b) Telephone the person and refresh your acquaintance
c) Drop by his/her office and hope he/she can see you

9. You have a really tight deadline and there is some very important information you need to get to the parties involved. What should you do?

a) Telephone them immediately and leave a voicemail
b) Send a detailed email promptly
c) Fax a copy of the pertinent information to their general office

10. An email message should be answered...

a) Within one hour
b) Within one day
c) Within twenty-four hours

(See answers at the end of this chapter.)

A. Email etiquette

Despite the sometimes intimidating technological air, email is just another way of communicating quickly and efficiently. It's not novel writing, on the one hand, but it's not a telephone or in-person discussion either, where communication is based on tone of voice and facial expression as much as it is on content. Here are some quick and easy tips for dealing with email etiquette.

- Don't be a novelist. Keep messages concise and to the point.

- Don't forget to check your own grammar and punctuation but don't correct errors in someone else's email. (unless you're the boss)

- Keep the formatting simple. Not everyone with access to email and the Internet has top of the line equipment and your message is lost if no one can't read it.

- Be careful with abbreviates. Some users have traded clarity for confusion by using this short from language. Here are some examples:

BCNU	Be seeing you
BTW	By the way
LOL	Laugh out loud
TTFN	Ta ta for now
TTYL	Talk to you later
EOM	End of message

- When necessary, use email "smiles." This will help alleviate misunderstandings and help convey the writer's emotions. Be careful though, these are NOT universal and could lead to a flam. Here are some examples:

:-)	Smiley face
:-(	Frown face
:-@	Scream face
:-*	Drunk face
:-D	Shock face
;-)	Wink or Sarcasm face

- Use appropriate salutations. For business use Mr., Ms., etc. for personal Dear is fine.

- Always make sure your letter is signed. You can create a signature in your email program that will automatically place your name, company, address, phone and email information at the bottom of every email.

- Always check to see it's there as it might not pop up when you're sending a reply. If it's not there, just use the "add signature" command from your toolbar menu.

- Do send a reply to maintain the "thread" or link between messages rather than start a new email message to respond. This keeps all parties abreast of the state of the conversation as well. Be careful, however, to check whom the reply is going to. It's easy, just double click on the name in the "to" box and a screen will pop up showing you the address where the message is going. This is extremely important because often forwarded messages will bounce back to the original sender and not necessarily to the person who forwarded you the message.

- Attach a file the sender can open. The other person may not have compatible software. An easy tip to remember is to save any word processing document in "rich text format" (just click "save as" and use the little menu at the bottom of the screen to select "rtf" instead of "Word" or "WordPerfect"). An rtf file can be opened by any word processing software program and it leaves the formatting intact. Make sure you let the receiver know this as well in the body of your email.

- Do not send large attachments. If it's bigger than a short word processing document, contact the receiver to find out if they want it, how big a file their system can handle, what kind of compression software they have, etc. If you are not familiar with these terms, get someone who knows computers to handle this for you. It's cute to send birthday cards, but not fun for the receiver when they crash his email program.

- Never send a resume as an attachment unless you've been requested to do so. Crashing a prospective employer's email system or sending a file he or she may think contains a virus is the number one way to ensure they never contact you!

B. Telephone etiquette

Communication tips and techniques to help you succeed in today's work place. The best etiquette advice of all regarding the telephone is-ANSWER IT. Stop for a minute and think about how much of your company's revenue is initially generated through the telephone. Sometimes it would make sense to have the telephone ring make the sound of a cash register to remind people in business just how important it is to actually answer the phone, and to do it happily, with the intention of selling themselves or something every time they pick it up.   There are several very annoying habits that we all recognize and hopefully will learn to avoid in our workplaces.

THE TALKAHOLIC: This violation is the worst.   The talkaholic takes telephone calls while talking or meeting with you.

He or she answers the phone and proceeds to have a lengthy conversation as if you weren't there! If you absolutely must take a call while you have a guest, tell the caller you have a guest and make the call as short as possible.

TALKUS INTERRUPTUS: This person barges into your office while you are on the phone and just starts talking to you! He ignores the fact that you are on the telephone.   Oh, it's not an emergency, either! It's just as rude to stand there not talking and listen to a conversation which you are not involved in as it is to interrupt.   Hint; keep your door closed while on important calls.

THE STALKER: This person paces back and forth like a starved wild animal while you're on the phone. The wild one wants to talk to you, so he/she hovers over you, shadows the door and makes you feel uncomfortable. Another type of stalker may leave you many, many messages and is unwilling to wait for a return call.

Keep in mind the following pointers for easier telephone relationships.

- **The phone is not an interruption.** Smile and pretend you have someone sitting across from you as you speak.

- **Return calls.** Phone calls should be returned the same business day if possible.

- **When leaving a message try to keep it simple.** Your name, company, time of call and brief reason for the call is sufficient. Leave the phone number at the beginning and the end of message so the person listening does not have to hear the whole message again.

- **Avoid phone tag.** To avoid phone tag leave a time for the person you are trying to reach so they will know the best time to reach you.

You may also want the person to just leave you a message or email you with an answer so the process of phone tag can be terminated.

- **Do not call an employee at home unless it is an emergency.** Home is the place people go to get away from work.   Remember, personal and business lives need to be separated for that balance to take place.

- **Wait by the phone.** When others do not return your calls, give them the benefit of the doubt and ask in your voicemail if they can leave you a better time to call or maybe someone else in their company who may be more appropriate to speak to. Change the message on your own system to let others know when you will be away and when you will be returning calls. This gives people an opportunity to call again or leave a message later in the week.

- **Limit your calls.** Do not call someone twice in one day unless on the message in the morning you indicated that you will reach them later in the day as you will be away from your desk. If someone doesn't call you back, chances are they are busy and will call when they can.

C. Cell phone etiquette

Any gadget that saves time and keeps you in the informational loop must be great, right? Cell phones certainly do have their advantages. But there are also disadvantages. In many instances, the convenience of technological interaction has overshadowed courtesy in modern communications. Here are some reasons these devices can be construed as rude and some guidelines for correct cell phone behavior.

- **Interruptions are rude.** A cell phone ringing while you are engaged in a conversation with someone is bad form. Either let the person you are speaking to know you are expecting a call and excuse yourself when it comes or shut the phone off.

- **They're listening.** Many people don't realize how distracting it is to others when they cannot help but hear your conversation. Talking on your cell phone while in line at the grocery or in the lobby of the doctor's office draws unnecessary attention and encroaches on the space and privacy of others. If you must make or take calls, do so in private. Among other places, cell phones do not belong in movie theaters, classrooms, special ceremonies, interviews or funerals.

- **Concentrate on the one you're with.** When you are engaged in face-to-face communication with someone, that person should have your undivided attention. If you are waiting for a call, you will not be focused on the person you are with. Similarly, if you have just completed a call, your attention will likely be on the communication which just transpired and again, not give your full attention to the person you are with.

D. Chapter summary

Technology has advanced quickly in today' ever-changing business world. Etiquette is still about respect for others: that will never change. Do not let the conveniences of modern gadgets displace courtesy and respect in daily communications.

Answers to self-assessment

1. a) It is not good manners to send via email, advertising, sale notices, chain letters or any other information that a person did not request be sent to him/her. It is particularly rude when this type of mail is sent at random by strangers with no return mail access.

2. b) Definitely send a handwritten note to their home address. Do not include a business card and do not discuss the particulars of the situation with co-workers. Keep this type of personal tragedy as personal as possible.

3. b) Give the client the benefit of the doubt. If you expressed yourself clearly, he/she would have understood the urgency of the situation. If he/she has not called, he/she probably does not have an answer. You should always tell a client in this situation that if you do not hear from him/her by a specific time, you will proceed accordingly. Chasing clients gives the impression of desperation or of aggression. Don't do it!

4. b) If at all possible, do not receive personal mail on your work computer. Ask your

friends to telephone you, write or email you at home.

5. c) Shut the phone off and apologize. Your superiors and co-workers deserve your full attention in this situation.   Unless your company policy is otherwise. Your phone is off during meetings.

6. c) It is always a good idea to let your feelings out but you're better off expressing them privately   first.   Often   telephone conversations, emails and even personal conversations take a negative tone when they occur under duress. When you are calm, you can present your case in a controlled, professional manner and still maintain your self-respect.

7. c)   Although interrupting is typically rude behavior, it is the lesser of two evils in this situation.   Give people an opportunity to recognize their lack of judgment and to extend repair behaviour when possible. Your integrity suffers if you do nothing and eavesdrop.

8. b) Telephone them first.   This is more personal and people may remember you by your voice. Email messages mean nothing if he receiver does not recognize the sender.

9. a) and b) If the information is very important, leave a message in more than one place just in case the person is not near the telephone or does not have access to his/her email.

10. b) Etiquette dictates that email messages should be responded to within one day of receipt. If you will be out of town or unable to return messages, you should relay this message to important associates and clients prior to your departure.

CHAPTER 5

PROFESSIONAL PRESENCE:
Judge not...

Appearance is an essential element in how others perceive us and, more importantly, how comfortable they feel in approaching us and doing business with us. How do we dress appropriately while maintaining our own sense of style? How do we dress professionally on a budget? How do we look approachable in formal business attire? How do we handle casual Fridays, and what exactly does "business casual" mean? How do we dress around our clients to make them comfortable?

At one of Civility Experts early training seminars, (to spice things up and to test our theory that image and first impression preface skills evaluation), we orchestrated the following scenario with two speakers: The first "guest speaker" arrived to discuss the importance of following the guidelines of proper email etiquette. Professionally dressed from head to toe and equally well spoken, his presentation was listened to with no signs of disinterest. Everything from his polished shoes to a close shave were all signs of self-respect and respect for the audience. He stood tall and confident and spoke clearly and concisely. The group had various questions, which were answered competently. The group was visibly impressed and a round of applause ended the successful session.

After lunch our next presenter arrived to speak about telephone etiquette. He wore tattered jeans, a faded dress shirt and a cartoon character tie. His shoes looked as though they were worn on the last climb up Everest and Grizzly Adams would have been proud of his five o'clock shadow. He sat slumped in a chair with his legs crossed at his ankles and his arms crossed in front of his chest. He mumbled at spoke so quietly that half the room was blatantly ignoring him and the other half was trying to lip-read. His professional presence had the group dismayed and disappointed. One woman pointed out that his inconsideration of the group was apparent from the minute he walked in the room.

Sure, it's not likely that a presenter would take things as far as Speaker #2 would- but you would probably agree that you've been in situations where it did seem that the presenter, or host, or VIP even, made little or not nearly enough effort to impress. How confident are you with your professional presence? Take the self-assessment and find out.

	True	False
1. Casual dress on Fridays means that my attitude and language can be casual too.		
2. Business casual means a man's shirt should have a collar.		
3. If a man does not have time to shave in the morning before work he should keep an electric razor in his desk drawer.		
4. It's perfectly okay to ask a well-dressed professional where he/she got his/her clothes and how much he/she paid.		
5. I can smoke in my own office even if the building is non-		

smoking		
6. If a co-worker is dressing inappropriately at work, I have a responsibility to tell him/her.		
7. If I have to attend a formal function in the evening, it is perfectly acceptable to wear my formal clothes during the day.		
8. It cannot be construed as sexual harassment if I comment on co-workers appearance whether man or woman.		
9. Everyone should know that good grooming is an intrinsic part of any workplace dress code.		
10. Chewing gum is a good habit to get into if you want to keep fresh breath.		

(See answers at the end of this chapter.)

A. What you see is what you think you're getting

The image we portray to our clients and associates involves many aspects of professional attributes. Our appearance and style are only a part of the equation.

Professional presence has a great deal to do with posture, facial expressions, gestures and subconscious movement. These are all intrinsic in how we are perceived by others. Here are some examples:

- **Attention...at ease:** How many times did your mother have to tell you...Sit up straight, keep your head up high, you're slouching! The way we sit and stand gives the people we are with an impression of how we feel about the situation we're in. By slouching in a chair or finding a wall to lean on as we conduct business, we give others the impression that we are indifferent or not interested or respectful of others. Our posture gives away how confident we feel, not to mention the health benefits of exceptional posture.

- **Take a look in the mirror:** Mirror, mirror on the wall are my facial expressions giving away it all? When in interviews or meetings, always consider the impact of your body language and facial expressions- often times what you don't say verbally says a lot!

- **Read me like a book:** Sighing, finger tapping on the boardroom table, and looking at your watch for the third time, sends a message of boredom and impatience. If a person is speaking look him/her in the eye, take notes and give your undivided attention.

- **Losing your cool when you're hot:** If you are unable to maintain your composure, take a breath and if possible, excuse yourself from the room or situation for a minute or two. When anger, impatience and irritation can crop up on you before you know it, reiterate the response or question and try listening or asking the person to explain. Remember you are a professional. If you feel your blood pressure rising, take a deep breath and keep calm.

- **Oh, you really are listening:** How many times have you wanted to wave a hand in front of someone's face and say aloud "Yoo hoo, anyone there?" As a good listener part of your responsibility is to nod occasionally or say the occasional yes or uh-huh. A polite person will not ask "Is anyone listening?" so effective listeners should let speakers see this by sending nonverbal listening cues.

- **Laughter is the best medicine...or is it?** That uncontrollable giggle or a hysterical outburst of hilarity, even a silly grin, can trigger suspicion and hard feelings during business meetings. If the person you sit next to turns you into a grade school classmate, find a new seat if you can't stop reminiscing. Sometimes, a polite chuckle during the client's gardening story or knee slapping during the company president's account of his fishing expedition are necessary, but be careful not to overdo it.

B. Groom and doom: Has casual Friday gone too far?

As times are changing and a more casual work environment has surfaced the question of what is suitable for work attire often becomes a discussion in the office. If you are setting the company dress code or finding the dress that most suits your corporate or business culture, casual does not mean carless. The way you present yourself to your clients, associates or co-workers sends them a message. This message can convey respect for others or confidence in yourself. The other side to this is a message of disrespect for the people you work with or equally unacceptable disrespect for yourself. That thrown together jeans and sweatshirt may be comfortable for you but if your client sees the casual dress as a sign of laziness or lack of time management, you won't be comfortable for long.

Casual is fine, careless is not. Follow these casual dressing tips for a look that says comfort and class:

- Always remove your hat when indoors. Even business casual means your baseball cap stays at home. Hats should not be worn in restaurants, meetings, church, receptions or places of work. It is a sign of disrespect. EXECEPTIONS: Indoor sporting events or for religious reasons.

- Do not wear open toes, sleeveless or revealing clothing in situations where a sit-down meal is being served or if you'll be in close physical contact with clients. This includes associates' homes, weddings, special events, the workplace or restaurants. It's just not good manners and you don't want the focus to be on your clothing or lack of clothing.

- "Casual" includes: khakis, sport shirts, sweaters, slacks, blouses and skirts. The kind of clothes you'd wear shopping or to the bank. Some people get casual confused with very informal or "play" clothes like tank tops, cut offs, bathing suits, gym clothes, yoga pants, or t-shirts which should only be worn around the house or for "play" and sports. Typically business casual means a tie is not required; however a collar is- as well as a firm fabric. Don't forget, casual clothes don't mean casual manners. Business people who dress business casual should remember that they will be in contact with clients who will make first impressions.

- In the business arena it is much safer to be overdressed than underdressed.

- Often when dressing, assess the role you will be playing that day. The level of formality depends on who you are interacting with and your responsibilities.

- Remember when accessorizing that the black leather belt you wear with your black pants probably won't go with your white spring dress. Be attentive to current styles as many people interpret being "on trend" fashion wise as being on trend business-wise as well.

- Less is more when it comes to make-up, jewelry and perfume. You can make a statement about your style without being excessive. Most business people do not appreciate "trends" like facial hair, piercings or body tattoos, so don't go out of your way to make statements or show off these very personal aspects of style. For typical business settings, hair color should be natural and neat and clean.

- Do not chew gum. It is noisy and looks bad. If you are worried about bad breath, brush your teeth often and carry mints.

Dressing properly is not only essential but imperative. You will be judged on how you appear and that includes what you wear!

C. Dress for success: Business dressing basics

There are no hard rules when it comes to professional dress. The situation will dictate style of dress along with the area you live or are working in, and certainly climate plays a role. For example chances are the dark, conservative suit you might wear to a formal business meeting in a downtown Toronto or New York boardroom would be a little out of place when meeting clients "in the field" e.g., with a livestock distributor in Dallas or a petroleum company in Calgary.

- **Dress to reflect your position:** The best advice, for the office, is to dress to reflect the position you are striving for. Mirroring someone who is respected and successful, whether it is with dress or attitude, can only help your career. If the person you directly report to wears a suit and you wear a pair of pants and a t-shirt, the next rung on the business ladder may be out of your reach. Time to go out and get a suit or two and change your image. The way you feel about yourself is reflected in the way you appear to others. Like it or not the clothes you wear will be judged by others. Have you ever noticed how great you feel when you take the time to dress appropriately? This feeling of confidence could carry you through to that promotion you've been waiting for.

- **Dressing on a budget:** Classic suits for men and women never go out of style and quality is the key. Trendy clothing may look sharp and make you feel stylish, for the period it is in style, but if your budget is limited, a few classic pieces will last longer and can easily be accessorized. Additional blouses, shirts, pants, etc. could also be added to update your wardrobe. Decide on what you need to purchase for your business wardrobe and do a little research. Often second-hand stores are full of classic pieces for those of us on a budget. Shop at times of the year when you know the sales for that season occur. Find out if one of your close friends who is similar in size would like to do a swap with you for a few days. You may also consider clearing out your closet of all those trendy, funky clothes in case you get the urge to wear those faded fatigue pants or that velour cowl neck sweater.

- **Dressing for clients:**   Working for or alongside a company during a project or contract also dictates style of dress. Consider who you may come in contact at work and dress to impress. It's easy enough to take a jacket off or remove a tie or some jewelry if you find you are too dressy, but it's difficult to improve your appearance if you show up in a golf shirt and jeans where everyone else is in a suit.

Making others comfortable is something you must consider as you dress each day. Have you looked around the place you will be spending time in for the duration? Observe what people are wearing and mirror the person who you will be spending the most time with. Respect for others and for oneself is key. It's not always necessary to completely change your image and buy a whole new wardrobe. Find clothing that makes you and others around you comfortable and not intimidated.

> **Appropriate footwear:** What you wear as an outfit needs to be complimented by the shoes that you choose each day. Platform, open-toed sandals, sling backs or runners do not have a place in an office where suits are

mandatory dress. For women, try to avoid dress pumps with casual pants and loafers with dresses. Comfort is important, especially if you are on your feet for extended periods of time.

Remember to always dress for success. As business people, there are times that the way you look can impact the amount of respect you receive from others. Be careful not to mirror the deportment disasters below:

THE UNDERTAKER: To onlookers, it would appear that this fellow co-worker has a part-time job at the funeral home. He is very serious and his attire is so very formal; always buttoned up and pinned down looking rather like an undertaker. Too much...lighten up please.

SUSIE CREAMTART: Suzie, Suzie you look like a floozie... Someone should tell little Miss Suzie not to wear her seamed stockings and gold lame blouses to work. And she wonders why she gets no respect, hmmmm!

STUCK IN THE SEVENTIES: This person is going to be 20 years old forever. The beehive or the wide ties give away his/her glory days. The suit fit him 30 pounds ago and she looks like she's wearing her daughter's high school graduation dress. Help!

D. What's your style? Maintaining a personal touch

When you look at the finished product, yourself, are you sending the right message to the people you are meeting? Your personal style is what makes you unique but it is the self-respect you exhibit that will make you a contender in today's workforce. Follow these tips for presenting yourself positively.

- **All that glitters:** Whether it is the crown jewels or your collection of costume jewelry, less is definitely more. If the jingling of your bracelets could summon the ghosts of pirates past you may decide to remove a few. When dressing, try to find one or two pieces that accentuate the clothes you choose for that particular day. The colorful broach or them socks that you can get away with wearing with your suit, would probably be inappropriate at a formal company function.

- **The sixth scent:** You may find yourself being sent far, far away to another place and time, if the perfume or cologne you wear arrives in the room before you do. Teary-eyed companions, associates with their hands over their noses and lonely coffee breaks are probably indicative that High Karate Harry has entered the building. Tone down your sixth scent and find a fragrance that matches your body chemistry- or avoid wearing fragrance altogether if you know you will be in close proximity with others.

- **The hand that you were dealt:** Your hand does not need to reflect all the colours of an artist's palette. Keep your nails clean, neat and well manicured and if you paint their nails, be subtle with colour choices and extras such as nail jewelry etc.

- **Good Afternoon...I would like you to meet my friend, the razor:** For those of you who do not know, facial hair grows 24/7 so even if you shaved before you went to bed, you'll probably be hairy again in the am and so have to shave again. A five o'clock shadow at ten in the morning might be "rugged" to some but for many at work it's just plain rough.

Keep a razor and cream in your desk drawer and if you are expecting a long day a second shave may be in order. Remember gentlemen, hair on the back of necks, on the tops of ears and "Bert and Ernie" brows all need to be addressed.

Other tips for successful dressing include:

- If you wear white tube socks to play squash at lunch, you'll need to change back to dark dress socks with your dress shoes

- Shoes should to be comfortable and fit properly. And, if the soles have come unglued and are slapping as you walk, for goodness sake find a glue gun.

- If the outfit you wear to the office can take you after work to the night club, no stops necessary, you might be wise to put a sweater over the sequins during work hours.

- Hair today, gone tomorrow...if you are still sporting your "Farrah Fawcett hairdo" (The

"Aniston" for you Gen X'ers) you might consider making a change. Consider your occupation- there's technically no rule that says only tattoo artists can wear Mohawks and orange feathers to work, but there's a reason you rarely see nurses and bankers doing it.

E. Chapter summary

In today's ever-competitive market, "business" usually means semi-formal business- in reference to verbal style, word choice, dress, demeanor, and etiquette. Business casual is becoming more acceptable but at no time are the following suitable:

Cut offs, tank or tube tops, baseball caps, sweat or windbreaker pants, torn anything is not cool at work. Let us also leave the advertising to billboards.

Slogans and statements are great at the beach but need to remain out of the office. Business situations dictate a professional presence and you are a representative of your company. The respect you feel for yourself and others is reflected in the way you dress, speak and conduct yourself.

Answers to self-assessment

1. False: Your attitude and speech style should be polished and professional at all times. Casual attire means only your clothing is casual.

2. True: Business casual means men should wear collars. T-shirts and v-neck's are not acceptable.   With the variety of shirts available with collars, there is no reason to wear a t-shirt. Please stay away from t-shirt that are for advertising purposes or ones that provide a statement or verse.

3. False: Your office desk is not your bathroom vanity.   At no time should clients or co-workers be witness to your personal grooming habits. This is not gender specific, no exceptions to this rule.

4. False: It is in very bad taste to ask anyone where he/she bought something or how much an item cost.

5. False: Smoking is unacceptable when you are with clients and if the office has a no smoking policy you should honor it

6. False: Unless you are the person's supervisor, keep your opinions to yourself.

7. False: It is unacceptable to wear formal clothes to the office unless the entire office is doing so for some specific reason. Bring the clothes with you or rearrange you schedule to make time to prepare for the function.

8. False: Check your company policy on harassment.   In business situations commenting on the appearance or dress of the opposite sex is not an appropriate thing to do.

9. True: Common sense dictates that you should go to work clean, neat and professionally dressed even if there is not a formal dress policy.

10. False: Chewing gum is a very rude and unsightly habit. Quickly and quietly take a mint instead.

Conclusion

Good manners are good business. Success in business depends on many factors, not the least of which is professional conduct. Professional conduct consists of everything from how a person presents him/herself outwardly-things like attire, demeanor, and tone of voice or listening skills-and extends to how a person exhibits attitude, respect, care and consideration for others.

Modern business etiquette guidelines provide a blueprint for behaving in business situations. The growing international marketplace together with an emphasis on both education and communication skills demand that men and women in business today acquire behaviors that set them apart from the competition. An understanding of how social behavior impacts business will enable them to make their way effortlessly through increasingly technological workplaces with their self-esteem, sense of humor and professional reputations intact.

A little courtesy never hurt anybody. Courtesy can only increase your self-confidence, your client base and subsequently your bottom line. Good Luck!

If you enjoyed this e-book, please visit www.civilitybooks.com to download other e-books such as "Beware the Tablemonsters" for children ages 5-10, or "Pass the Promotion Please" and "P's and Q's for Profit" for adults in business.

You can learn more about Civility Experts by visiting www.civilityexperts.com *and you can take online courses including Civility Train the Trainer Certification courses and a free mini course on How Civility Increases Retention, Engagement and Profitability by visiting* www.civilityexpertsonline.com

www.ingramcontent.com/pod-product-compliance
Lightning Source LLC
Chambersburg PA
CBHW060614200326
41521CB00007B/766